Anonymous

Overland to Klondike Through Cariboo, Ominica

Anonymous

Overland to Klondike Through Cariboo, Ominica

ISBN/EAN: 9783744760911

Printed in Europe, USA, Canada, Australia, Japan

Cover: Foto ©Andreas Hilbeck / pixelio.de

More available books at **www.hansebooks.com**

OVERLAND TO KLONDIKE.

THROUGH CARIBOO, OMINICA, CASSIAR, AND LAKE TESLIN.

THE POOR MANS ROUTE

1898

A BEATY DEL.

J. W. FRANKS & SONS, PRINTERS, PEORIA.

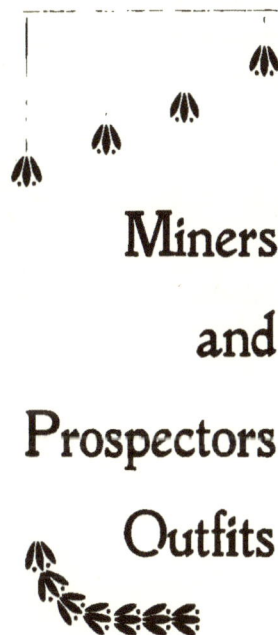

PREFACE

*

T HE many letters of inquiry received of late by the residents of Ashcroft and those residing along the Cariboo Road, at Clinton, the 150, Soda Creek, and Quesnelle, shows that a knowledge of the actual condition of the overland route to the Gold Fields of British Columbia, the Northwest Territories, and the Yukon, is being eagerly sought for by the public. To meet these inquiries, this volume is published.

Respectfully,

The British Columbia Mining Journal

ASHCROFT, BRITISH COLUMBIA
DEC. 10TH, 1897

HARVEY, BAILEY & CO.

CARIBOO FORWARDING AGENT

ASHCROFT, B. C.

OVERLAND.

ROM Ashcroft to Quesnelle is 220 miles over a splendid Government Stage road, semi-weekly mail stages convey her Majesty's mails from Ashcroft to interior points the year around. Passengers are also carried by the British Columbia Express Company, who have the mail contracts for that section. At Quesnelle, the Fraser River is crossed, there being a steam ferry that crosses passengers and horses at reasonable rates. From this point it is about 300 miles by the old telegraph trails to Hazelton on this Skeena River. From Hazelton to Telegraph Creek on the Stickine is about 200 miles, and from Telegraph Creek to Lake Teslin is about 120 miles, making the entire distance by trail from Quesnelle where the Overland Route proper begins, about 620 miles. Add the 220 miles of stage road to Ashcroft and you have a total of 840 miles. This trail cut out so many years ago, has been in constant use since, but some sections of it, more particularly that from Hazelton to Telegraph Creek has not been used to the extent that it was in early days. The consequence is that in many places, trees have fallen across the trail and those traveling through would rather go around a fallen tree than to cut it out. This makes traveling for small parties slow, but a large party could easily clear out all obstructions of this kind and scarcely delay a pack train an hour. Of feed there is an abundance, from early in May until in November. Blue joint and wild pea vine growing in profusion. The Provincial government has promised to have a party of men at work on the Overland Trail at the earliest possible time in the Spring and not later than March to cut out the fallen timber and put it in good condition for the many thousands that will pass through in the early spring. This route is very appropriately called the poor man's route to the Klondike. With a few cayuses, which can be obtained for little money and a year's supply of provision, a gun and fishing tackle, a man can leave Ashcroft and reach any point he pleases in the Northwestern Gold Fields, and will need to pay out scarcely a dollar. A little help, perhaps, in ferrying or swimming a couple of rivers, which can always be obtained from the Indian villages near the fords or crossings. If he decides towards Fall so to do, he can sell his pack animals for which there is always a demand in the vicinity of Telegraph Creek, after getting his supplies to Lake Teslin, buy a few hundred feet of lumber at the saw mill at the head of the Lake, build his boat and load it, and from the time he leaves until he reaches Dawson City, he encounters no bad waters, except that at Five Fingers after the junction of the Hootalinqua, the outlet of the lake with the Lewis River, and the Five Fingers can be run with a loaded boat with safety if in charge of a competent boat man.

The country passed through on this Overland Trail is gold bearing nearly the entire distance. The immense gravel mines of Cariboo, one mine alone the Cariboo Hydraulic, produces an average of over $2,000 per day during the season, and which has sent down several washups of $75,000 to $85,000 for a single run. The old Creek beds that have never been bottomed, but known from their situation and the fact that the benches are rich, contain perhaps as great an amount of gold as world famed Williams or Lightning Creeks, out of which more than $40,000,000 have been taken since their first discovery, 1859. The Golden River Quesnelle, from whose bars fortunes have been rocked, and on which thousands of Chinese have, for the past twenty years, been rocking, they work a few seasons and by their thrift and industry accumulate a few thousand dollars, and satisfied, go back to the flowery kingdom to spend the balance of their days in luxury and ease, their places being taken by other Celestials who repeat the performance. The country being thus stripped of its gold with little in the way of an equivalent. The Horse Fly mines, a ten stamp quartz mill, its hydraulic elevators, and deep diggings now producing, but the output to be much increased in the near future, immense works on Williams Creek by the Cariboo Gold Field's Company, the Antler Creek Mines, Slough Creek Mine, Willow River, Quesnelle Forks, and vicinity, the Montreal, the Beaver Mouth, and many other promising large hydraulic mines soon to be opened upon a large scale, the Fraser River Mines, and other sections too numerous to mention, all of which goes to show that the section first discovered to be gold bearing in 1859, and well named Golden Cariboo, is yet a promising field for capital. It is not, as a rule, at this time, a poor man's diggings, as machinery is required to handle the water from the deep shafts along the creek beds or in placing the immense hydraulic machinery, nevertheless, men do, sometimes, strike surface diggings, where gold can be taken out without a large capital. As a rule there is plenty of work at fair wages, $2 00 to $3.00 and board are paid, and it will be remembered that this section is so close to rail transportation, that living is comparatively cheap. The Overland Trail strikes north from Cariboo across the Fraser and past the Ominica Mines. In this well known district, several large mining companies are at work installing large plants. The 43d Mining & Milling Co., of Ottawa, Canada, have worked from sixty to eighty men each season for the past three years, and the Victoria Consolidated Mining Co. about an equal number The mines owned by these companies are on Slate, Manson, and Germanson Creeks. Individual miners are working in this section, and some are said to be making from $10.00 to $30.00 per day to the man. There is a large portion of this district not yet thoroughly prospected. It is but a short journey from the Ominica Mines to the head waters of the Peace River. On the Parsnip, Smoky, Nation and other streams, large dredging plants are being placed, and that section will be brought well to the front in 1898. A rich strike was reported late this season on some creeks that are tributary to the Nation River, and many claims were located, but too late in the season to get absolute information of the extent and value of the new finds. There is, however, no question but that there are good mines to be found in this section; at least, this is the belief of those who are thoroughly informed of the conditions and lay of the land.

Of Cassiar and vicinity, it is sufficient to say that many millions have been taken out since 1870, and work is still being prosecuted. Late this season a number of Chinamen came down from Victoria with from $5,000 to $30,000 each as the result in some cases, of a few years work. Owing to the isolated location on the Cassiar Mines and the extreme high cost of living, combined with the comparatively short season, the country was never thoroughly pros-

STEAMER CALEDONIA ON STICKEEN RIVER

pected, and there is a chance for thousands of prospectors in to the North and East of Lake Teslin and down the Pelly and Hootalinqua Rivers. This section of the country, probably 500 miles in length, and from 200 to 300 miles in width, is entirely unprospected. There is no man in the West better informed, in a general way, of Northern British Columbia, than Mr. R. H. Hall, of Victoria, who has been for thirty years in the employ of the Hudson Bay Company, and for many years in charge of the trading posts of the Company for British Columbia, and as such agent visits each season all of the Northern posts. Mr. Hall said to the writer a few weeks since: "I believe that as great or greater mines than those of Klondike, will be found in the section of country lying North of Cassiar and East of Lake Teslin, and reaching down to Stewart River and Klondike. This section I saw a small portion of last season, and was much impressed with it as a gold country, but few, if any, men have ever crossed it, and hundreds of square miles have never been seen or crossed by Indians or whites. It seems to me from the favorable location and formation that a little of the golden treasure this section contains, has spilled down through Cassiar, and at the other end of this track is Klondike, but the great body of gold mining country, is lying between, and mines of immense value will be found in this unexplored territory in the near future."

The New York World Sent a Special Correspondent, Mr. W. M. Pindell, to Investigate This Route, and He Had This to Say in an Article Published in the World, Oct. 24th.

Put in a nutshell, the route in question begins at Ashcroft on the Canadian Pacific Railroad; follows the Cariboo stage route to Quesnelle; from Quesnelle follows the trail of the old Great Western overland telegraph line to Hazleton; from Hazleton to Telegraph Creek on the Stickeen River, and from the Stickeen River to Lake Teslin. Lake Teslin is the very headwaters of the Yukon River, and from its extreme upper end, where the travelers will land, it will be an easy matter to transport themselves, their horses and their supplies by flatboat to Dawson City or to any other point along the Yukon where they may think there is a better chance of finding gold.

All this without the aid of a map, and without information concerning the wide stretch of country to be traversed, is very vague and meaningless. It requires, however, only a glance at the map to grasp the general features of the route, and as I have just returned from a journey over a part of it, and as I have talked with people who have traversed much more of it, I am able to supply information which will be common enough no doubt a year hence, but which at present is comparatively little known.

Starting at Ashcroft, which is a little trading town on the Canadian Pacific Railroad, somewhere between 200 and 300 miles east of Vancouver, I went to Soda Creek, 165 miles due north, in the old-fashioned six-horse stage coach which makes the journey twice each week. The road is in excellent condition, and there are capital inns at intervals of thirty miles all along the route. It is over this road, of course, that the Klondike caravans of the near future will be passing, and although it runs for miles along the sides of high mountains, it is nowhere dangerous to a rider or driver of any ordinary degree of skill or caution. At Soda Creek you have an option of two routes. You may continue on the stage coach, or you may take the comfortable little steamer Charlotte down the Fraser River to Quesnelle. The distance is sixty miles.

Now all of this is an old and well-known road, and in that section of the country—a road over which commercial and other travelers think no more of going than they do over any of the beaten tracks of the Eastern States. But it is at the end of this 220 mile journey that the real trip to the Klondike begins. Quesnelle is in reality "the jumping-off place"—the last white settlement until you reach the Skeena River at Hazleton, 300 miles away.

You cross the Fraser River at Quesnelle by a steam ferry boat, and then, only a few hundred yards from the river's brink, you plunge into the great silent wilderness of lofty pines and rugged mountains, which continues unbroken for hundreds of miles to the north. There is an interesting bit of romance about your road after leaving Quesnelle. It follows what is known as the old "Telegraph Trail"—a great swath 120 feet wide cut straight through the forest, and intended originally to reach to Behring Straits, opposite the continent of Asia. It is the scar left by a great commercial failure, this old telegraph trail. It is at once a scar and a memorial to the persistence and genius of Cyrus W. Field. People who jeered at Mr. Field's idea that electric signals could be transmitted by a wire laid under the Atlantic Ocean, set about building a telegraphic line to Europe, while Mr. Field was tinkering with what they regarded as his day dreams. So they plunged into the great Northwest woods to build a line to Behring Straits, and so to Asia, and so on again to the civilization of Western Europe. But while they were still cutting timber, Mr. Field got to sending telegraph messages between New York and London, so they shouldered their axes and came out of the woods, leaving the telegraph trail behind them as a monument to the hundreds of thousands of dollars they had sunk in the enterprise.

The great 120 feet wide swath is now much overgrown, of course, but through the center of it there runs a wide, smooth path, over which I myself rode a great many miles; and when I say that it is not an uncommon thing for a man to ride a bicycle from Ashcroft to Quesnelle, and that the telegraph trail from Quesnelle northward would make a smoother and better bicycle path than the stage road from Quesnelle southward, I do not know that anything further need be said about this particular stretch of the poor man's road to the Klondike. Furthermore, I can say, as bearing upon the condition of this part of the road, that Mr. J. D. Devereux, a young surveyor, left Quesnelle on September 7th last, and made the trip alone to Hazelton — 300 miles — in thirteen days. He had two horses, and he writes me that he was delayed a good deal by fallen timber.

After leaving Hazleton, which is a Hudson Bay Company's trading post, the first stage of the journey northward is fifty miles to Nasse River, which you cross by an Indian ferry. Then you are only 150 miles from Telegraph Creek and the Stikeen River, with a good trail all the way, and Indian ferries for all the streams of any size or difficulty. From Telegraph Creek there is a fine Government trail over the route surveyed for a railroad by the Canadian Pacific Company, a distance of 120 miles, to the head of Teslin Lake. Here the worst part of the journey ends, for getting down the lake and from the lake down the Yukon River to Dawson City, is only a matter of plain boating. It is not unlikely that a steamboat will be plying on Teslin by next spring, and, even if that is not the case, the construction of flatboats capable of carrying travelers with their horses and supplies is a simple matter, with all the fine timber there is at hand for the purpose.

From this general outline it will be seen that there is here open a perfectly safe and comparatively easy route to the Klondike gold fields which heretofore has not been in any of the columns of matter which have been printed in newspapers and books since the excitement over the gold discoveries began. It is not to be understood, however, that the people along the route — the people who inhabit the region between Ashcroft and Quesnelle—are not alive to the fact that at no very distant day their country is destined to be on the line of a much-traversed route to the North. But the Canadians are nothing if not a conservative race, and the Canadians of British Columbia are no exception to the rule. Had such an opening to a country which so many thousands desire to reach been through any part of the United States, it is perfectly safe to say that steam and electric railways, as well as steamboats for the navigable waters, would already have been far advanced in construction. The trail from Quesnelle to Hazleton and Telegraph Creek has been traversed for years by carriers of the Hudson Bay Company, and the route from there on to Lake Teslin and the head waters of the Yukon, is equally familiar to hundreds of surveyors and adventurous spirits who have traversed it time and again. That it is a perfectly clear, open route to the Klondike has been generally commented upon by the people up there, but there has been what in the United States would be considered a curious apathy in turning the fact to profitable account; not, however, that there are wanting men up there with a keen appreciation of the situation. Dr. F. S. Reynolds, publisher of the *British Columbia Mining Journal*, was an early advocate of this overland route, and has done much work in connection with it. Senator James Reid and Representative Adams, of Quesnelle, two of the leading men of the province, have also taken much interest in the matter. It is obvious that people on the coast are not going to exert themselves to point out how the argonauts may give them a wide berth on the way to the gold fields. So with this, and the languid attitude of the Fraser River people, this excellent overland route to the Klondike has been totally overlooked by all who thus far have gone or talked of going to the gold fields.

The general plan to be followed by those who may contemplate experimenting on this route is very simple. They should be in Ashcroft about the middle of April, and then buy their supplies. A party of four or five would probably get along best. Each person will need two cayuses, and cayuses are tough little Canadian horses. They are very cheap in Ashcroft. Two good ones may be had for $50. One would be used, of course, as a beast of burden, and the other to be ridden. By starting in the early spring, good grass and feed for the animals will be found all along the route from the starting point to the Yukon.

Supplies, likewise, can be bought to advantage at Ashcroft, although they may be renewed at Quesnelle, Hazleton and Telegraph Creek. As for the time occupied in the journey, it may be roughly estimated, as the conditions now are, at about six weeks. As the route becomes known, and as the British Columbia people awaken to the situation, the trails and the river crossings, and the steamboat facilities will be so improved that this time limit from Ashcroft to Dawson City will be much diminished.

And right here in this connection it may be said that a very important

PARTY LEAVING TELEGRAPH CREEK FOR THE GOLD FIELDS EAST OF LAKE TESLIN.

feature of this route lies in the fact that the travelers will arrive at their destination with a very valuable property in the horses which have carried them there, and which will be sold readily, up where means of transportation are in such demand, for many times their original cost.

And a further very important point is that the country, all the way up, will not only supply the horses with fodder, but will give all the food in the way of game that is wanted for the travelers themselves. Wild fowl and fish are in bewildering abundance all along the route. Furthermore, plenty of Indians will be met with, and, if they are properly treated, they will be found obliging and very useful. There are several Indian villages between Quesnelle and Telegraph Creek; and, in fact, all the way over to the head waters of the Yukon.

But the most important feature of all lies in the fact that there is gold all the way up from Fraser River north. The route lies right along the great gold and silver belt which extends from Mexico to Alaska. Chinamen manage to make a profit by gold washing right in the vicinity of Quesnelle, although that region was pretty well cleaned up by the forty-niners who followed the gold thus far up into the north. But very valuable finds have recently been reported from the Skeena River, and the Argonauts would find promising fields for prospecting all the way on to the Yukon, and might strike their fortune even before they reached the golden Klondike.

But, even if they did push on to the Klondike, they would arrive there pretty well-seasoned pilgrims, and not the bewildered, flabby tenderfeet who are dumped with their year's supplies on the bank of the Yukon, with no means of transportation to get to their destination, and utterly unbroken-in to the rough life before them.

Mr. W. H. Griffin, who made the trip from the head of Lake Teslin to Dawson and return last fall, made the following statement to me:

"Teslin Lake is about 150 miles long and averages about three miles in width. A large but sluggish river empties into it at its upper end, and here the Indians have their canoe cache, where they leave their boats during their absence while going to and coming from Juneau on their annual trips to dispose of their furs.

"Here, at the head of the lake, we built our boats and started on our prospecting. There are three streams emptying into the lake from the north. Two of these, the Oklohene and the Netticene, are quite large and very swift. There is only one river running in from the south. There is no part of the lake that is not navigable for light draught steamers, and the greater part of it is extremely deep. In some places we were unable to find bottom with a 100-foot line. The shores are for the most part rocky and precipitous, but beautiful camping places can be found along the north shore. As you approach the lower end of the lake the banks are of clay, quite high, and coming down into deep water.

"The lake gradually grows narrow, and before you are aware of its proximity you are entering the Hootalinqua River, which is the outlet of this large body of water. We expected to find a narrow river, but instead of that there was no current to speak of for some miles. As we proceeded down the river, which is 180 miles long, the speed of the current increased until it was running at the rate of about five miles an hour. The Hootalinqua is perfectly safe for any rowboat, and navigable for light-draught steamers through its entire length. The same can be said of the rest of the route to Forty-Mile

with one exception. This exception is the Five-Finger Rapids, which any
boat can run with ordinary caution without unloading.

"While on the lake, we met Mr. J. Colbreath, who had just come through
from Telegraph Creek with his pack train of thirteen horses. He informed
me that the trail was in good condition."   W. M. PINDELL.

The Following Descriptive Letter is from A. L. Poudrier, Dominion Land Surveyor of Robson, B. C., Under Date of October 6th, 1897:

The government of British Columbia has spent many thousands of
dollars during the last eight or nine years in exploring and surveying the
northern portion of the Province, and, although the work is not quite completed, the portion more nearly related to the Yukon country is fairly well
known.

Having been employed during several years at that work, it has been
my good fortune to travel many times through that great valley which begins at the Fraser river and reaches the source of the Yukon, that is, Teslin
Lake. The valley of the Yukon is simply a continuation of that cut, and,
no doubt, in the far ages, this king of streams was far longer than it now is.

As many persons intend to go to Alaska in the spring, starting from
Washington and going via Ashcroft, a description of the route may prove of
interest. I will say nothing of the first part of the road, as Ashcroft may be
reached either by rail or overland from Washington.

There is a first class wagon road, 220 miles in length, from Ashcroft to
Quesnelle Mouth. This road is in perfect order, and a stage line, as regular
in its time card as any railway, makes the round trip every week. The land
is fairly settled along the whole distance, and farm houses and regular
stopping places are met at short intervals. For those who travel with their
own pack horses, free feed is plentiful all along.

Quesnelle Mouth is a small town on the banks of the Fraser river. It
has a first class grist mill, where flour is nearly as cheap as in Spokane.
For many things needed on a long trip to the north, such as fur robes for
bedding, moccasins and duffel (a thick woolen cloth, made especially for
Indian trading), no other place equals that little town.

The Fraser has to be crossed here, and there is a good ferry. One has
now reached the gold country of the Cariboo excitement, and at Quesnelle
the banks of the Fraser have been washed and re-washed. This, too, is the
beginning of the old telegraph trail, and in many places the wire can still be
seen strung up or lying along the wayside.

The country from Quesnelle to the Nechaco valley and Fraser Lake, a
distance of 150 miles, may be generally described as a rolling country, with
no high mountains, and covered with a growth of small poplars, birch and
black pine, nearly all of second growth; only a few tall trees of the old
original forest are to be seen.

The trail crosses many small streams and follows the banks of numerous
lakes, where rich meadows and open glades give the richest of food for
animals at nearly all parts of the trail. When the water is high, one stream,
called the Chillacco, or Mand river, gives trouble. That is, at the end of

June or early in July. Only one other stream of consequence is met; that is the Blackwater, and it is crossed on a good bridge.

On reaching the Nechaco valley, rich meadows—which will be the farms of the future—are traversed by the trail along beautiful lakes, where many Indians are living. The Nechaco is crossed to reach Fort Fraser, a Hudson Bay post and a large Indian village.

From Fort Fraser the trail follows the south bank of Lake Fraser for twelve miles, through a rich, rolling, park-like country; and the stream emptying Lake Francais into Lake Fraser is crossed near the village of Nadina. The ford is easy. The Indians in this part are called "Carriers," and are good, hospitable and honest.

From Nadina the trail follows the valley of the Endako, which empties into the Stellaco. It is a wide valley with much open land and bunchgrass, good for farming and grazing.

The distance from Stella to Hazleton, on the Skeena, is 160 miles. After reaching the source of the Endako, the trail enters the valley of the Bulkley or Hagwilget river, falling into the Skeena. This valley is similar to the Endako, with broad meadows, beautiful open grassy slopes, light park-like woods, full of small fruit in season. The streams and many lakes are full of fish—salmon, trout, char and two or three other kinds. Small game is plentiful all the way from Quesnelle. Grouse, ducks and geese are abundant in season, while rabbits and deer are scarce. Bears are most common, especially in the Endako and Bulkley valleys, where black, brown and grizzly bears are met every day.

This road is not far from the Omenica gold fields, and gold is found on almost every creek along the trail from Lake Fraser, though no very rich ground has ever been struck. It is quite possible, however, that some of the small streams might give good results to the prospector.

Hazleton is a Hudson Bay post, Indian agency and mission post. The Hudson Bay Company's steamer, Caledonia, makes occasional trips from the sea. Supplies of all kinds can be purchased at this point, as it is partly the rendezvous of the miners working in Omenica. The river can be crossed with canoes, and the horses have to swim. Horses are fairly abundant here, nearly every Indian owning one or more.

Hazleton was the last place where the wire was stretched for the telegraph company. From here the trail follows the Skeena for twelve miles to the Indian village of Kyspyox, and there two routes can be taken—one, the longest, follows the Skeena to the Indian village of Kuldo and then goes northerly to the Chean-Wean, a branch of the Naas river. The first part of this trail—that is, as far as Kuldo—is fairly well traveled.

For a big expedition the better road is to follow the Kyspyox river to its source. From there the valley is occupied by two branches of the Naas river, the Koniscees and Chean-Wean. Thence the trail follows two branches of the Iskoot, a large stream falling into the Stickeen. The main branch of the Iskoot is called the Ningumsa. From this stream the trail strikes a small river called the First South branch of the Stickeen. At the mouth of this the Stickeen is crossed by swimming the horses. Telegraph creek and Glenora are quite close.

From Fraser Lake to Glenora the distance is 278 miles. The trail was never cut wide, as the portion after leaving Quesnelle is seldom used, and in many places barely visible. For a large party with men ready to cut a fallen

QUESNELLE RIVER BRIDGE

tree once in a while or to clear a thicket of underbrush, it would cause little delay, but for a small party it would be a serious loss of time. The country here is similar in appearance to the portion just described. Game is plentiful, feed common and open land often met with.

The navigation from the sea on the Stickeen to Glenora is easy, and there are, I believe, two steamers running continually. Telegraph creek is a good point to obtain supplies, and it was easy to find packers there, but one cannot say how the excitement and rush to the Yukon may have affected the place. From Glenora to Teslin Lake, by the pack trail was 130 miles. They are now cutting a wagon road and surveying a railroad for the Canadian Pacific, and large trains will be employed all winter freighting goods and machinery to the lake, and this winter will be a very busy season.

The country north of the Stickeen is perhaps a little more wooded than further south, but, nevertheless, food for horses is very abundant. Gold is found on nearly every stream, and on the Thulton and Dodedonto rich prospects have been located.

Teslin Lake is a very beautiful sheet of water, from two to six miles in width and about eighty miles in length. The shores are not high and are generally covered with the same short growth of trees which characterizes all of the interior plateaus. A sawmill has lately been built at the lake, and several steamers will be constructed during the winter.

The navigation from the lake to Dawson is open, there being only one rapid which is not of much importance.

The river coming out of Lake Teslin is called the Hootalinqua, and then the Lewes to the point where the Pelly reaches it at old Fort Selkirk, where it takes the name of Yukon. I believe this is wrong. The Hootalinqua and Lewes are by far the largest feeders of the Yukon; they are also in the same line of direction. Therefore, according to the rules of physical geography it should be called the Yukon, and Lake Teslin is its source.

Two noted gold fields are known in New Caledonia—the Omenica, north of Lake Fraser, and the Cassiar, which begins at Telegraph creek. Large amounts have been taken from this locality. In Ominica powerful companies have started hydraulic mining on a large scale, and, no doubt, the same will soon be done in Cassiar. People with experience in that line and with sufficient capital do not need to go as far as the Yukon. Cassiar offers as rich a prize as Klondike to the hydraulic miner.

Large tracts are not yet prospected at all, even for placers, and nothing whatever has been done in the line of quartz mining. It is known that rich deposits of galena ore occur on the Skeena, and rich copper ore is to be found on the Stickeen and on Lake Teslin. Native copper has been mined for ages by the Indians from this locality and has been hammered into shields used for currency, which can yet be obtained.

There is no doubt that the road from the sea to Telegraph creek, by the Stickeen, will be largely used next spring; and as the great field for prospecting will be the upper Yukon, Lake Teslin should be a busy spot next year.

For those who wish to take horses or cattle, the way I have described from Quesnelle offers no dangers of any sort, no difficulties. Far from it; it is one of the most pleasant trails to travel, and I have remembrance of

ON THE FRASER RIVER

many happy days employed riding daily along and camping at night loaded
with small game. With such a climate during spring, summer and autumn,
it is easy to forgive a few weeks of cold weather.

A. L. POUDRIER,
Dominion Surveyor.

Thomas Hamilton, to whom we are under obligations for much valuable information, says:

He was for seventeen years an employe of the Hudson Bay Company in
that section, viz.: Stuart's Lake, for four years, at Nechaco River, and for
some years a trader at Fort Connelly. During Mr. Hamilton's time many
bands of cattle were successfully driven into Telegraph Creek and the Cassair
mines. The route, Mr. Hamilton says, is through a country abounding in
feed, and the trail is easy for packing or herding cattle. From Telegraph
Creek the new trail to Teslin Lake will put interior British Columbia within
easy drive of the Yukon markets. No other route offers the inducement for
overland travel to the Klondike that the Cariboo-Cassair-Teslin Lake route
does. Thousands will travel it next season. They will buy their pack animals
in Ashcroft and begin the journey here. All along the route they can restock
and resupply if they wish at Telegraph Creek, and further, they can spend
their time profitably in prospecting the creeks and rivers on their way, and
may strike another Klondike before going many hundred miles, and Teslin
Lake, 760 miles from Quesnelle by trail, is bound to be a great mining section,
so say all authorities.

As many inquiries have been made as to whether a portion of this route could be made by water to advantage, the following letters are of interest:

*Extracts from a letter received from Senator James Reid, of Quesnelle, to
the editor of the Journal:*

"I have yours of the 14th, and will comply with request as correctly as I
know how. The charge by steamer as far as she can go at present, viz.:
Soda Creek to Cottonwood Canyon, is one cent per pound, but in 100 ton lots
could make some reduction. From thence it can be taken by boats or canoes
up to the head of North Tatlah Lake, say about 300 miles from Cottonwood
Canyon. This latter would cost about eight cents per pound. This will
leave you in the middle of the Ominica country, and from thence via Fort
Connelly by land to the Cassiar mines is about 200 miles.

"I may say that the Dominion Government has an engineer now up
examining the Fraser, Nechaco and Stuart Rivers, with a view to their being
made navigable for steamers, there being only three or four points which
need clearing out in the whole 300 miles to Buckley House, at the head of
North Tatlah Lake, and as soon as these places are made navigable, the
North British Navigation Company intend placing steamers suitable for the
trade of that route.

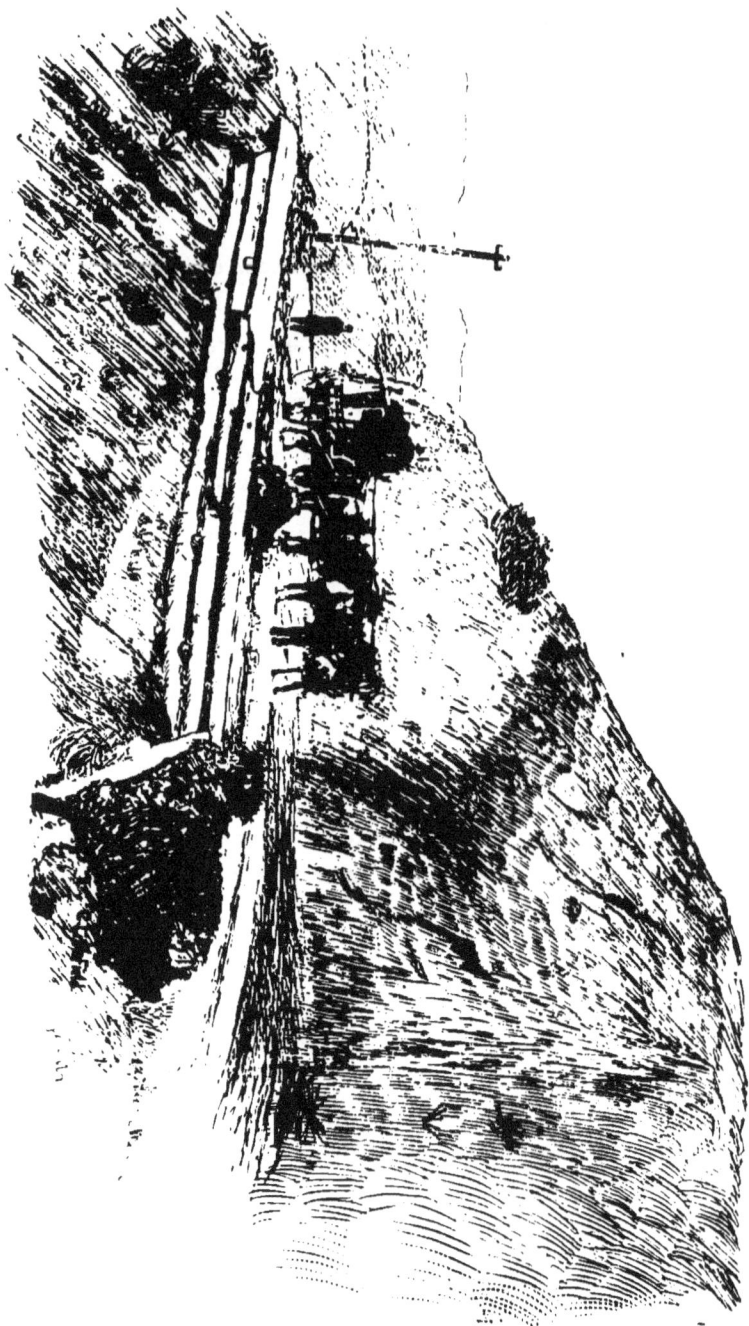

CARIBOO STAGE ENROUTE

" Meantime, my idea of going into the Yukon, which is, I presume, the objective point, would be to bring goods to Soda Creek by team or train (freight this season two and one-half cents per pound), thence by steamer, which would land freight on either side of the river at Quesnelle for half a cent per pound (distance 60 miles), and from thence by pack animals by the telegraph trail to Telegraph Creek and Teslin Lake. The cost, distance and time would be about as follows:

DAYS.	PLACES.	MILES.		COST.
12	Ashcroft to Soda Creek....................	163		2½c
1	Soda Creek to Quesnelle	60		½c
16	Quesnelle to Hazleton	240	say	6c
13	Hazleton to Telegraph Creek	200	"	5c
10	Telegraph Creek to Teslin Lake...........	120	"	3c
52		783		17

"This would be about the ordinary time for a pack train to travel. of course, going light, faster time could be made.

" Another route to go north is directly up the Fraser and Giscomb Portage, distance from Cottonwood Canyon about 115 miles, thence across a portage to Summit Lake, seven miles, thence by small boats or canoes via McLeod Lake down the Parsnip river to its junction with the Peace River, thence up the Findlay Branch to near the Liard River tributaries, which lies between the Ominica country and tributaries of the Yukon River. Any of the routes mentioned are within the gold bearing zone lying in a direct northwest line from Cariboo to Klondike.

" The only obstructions to navigation on the Fraser river are Cottonwood Canyon and Fort George Canyon, and I think if the latter were improved somewhat, the former could be managed as it is, so that steamers could run from Soda Creek to Giscomb Portage, say 195 miles, at a cost for freight of say not over three cents a pound."

From P. C. Dunlevy, Soda Creek, B. C.

"In answer to yours of the 14th ultimo will say: There are but two places in the Fraser River where boats heavily laden should be lightened of part of their loads, first the Cottonwood canyon, at certain seasons, is unsafe to take a boat very heavily laden through. About one-half of the load should be taken out and packed around the canyon half a mile; there is a good wagon road around. Second, Fort George canyon, where the same should be done. Then you have plain sailing to the head of Tatlah Lake by going up the Nechacc and Stuart Rivers into Stuart's Lake, thence up Tatchie River a distance of fifteen miles to Lake Trombley, thence up Little River a distance of twelve miles into Lake Tatlah which is about seventy miles long.

"Should you desire to follow the Fraser there are no obstacles in the way of boating until you pass Giscomb, or say about eighty miles above Fort George. There is no place along either of these streams one could not unload on the banks except in the canyons. I have had goods delivered at the head of Tatlah Lake for six cents per pound. This was twenty years ago. No doubt it could be done cheaper now. If there was a trail from some point near the head of Tatlah Lake into the Stickeen River it would pass by the headwaters of the Findlay and Omenica Rivers. The country, I am creditably informed, is sparsely timbered, gravel hills with much quartz showing in many places, and while no prospecting has been done there, gold has been found by men passing through the country. There is scarcely a shadow of doubt but that rich mines could be found throughout the entire distance to Cassiar, as many of the bars in the Findlay have paid well, some as high as $50 per day to the man, and in every instance the bars grow richer the nearer you approach the heads of the streams. It would be of great benefit to British Columbia and the entire Dominion if the government would remove the obstacles in the river this winter and make it navigable through to Tatlah Lake. The Provincial Government could not spend a little money to a greater advantage to the Province than opening the trail from Tatlah through this section of country by the head of the Findlay and Ominica. I feel quite sure they would be amply repaid in revenue from this section in a very short time. By removing the obstacles to navigation in the Fraser and Nechaco Rivers, steamers would be enabled to lay goods within twenty-five miles of the Ominica, whence they could have down stream to the Ominica mines, Germansen and many other streams where gold has been found in paying quantities. I say nothing about the route up the Fraser to Giscomb Portage thence over the divide into the Parsnip River, as I presume you care nothing about that country. The route by Nechaco is in almost a direct line with Cassiar and Klondike. By all odds the best and cheapest way for persons going to the Klondike would be to cross the Fraser here and follow the trail via Fraser Lake and Hazleton to Telegraph Creek until navigation is possible. I have traveled over it as far as Fraser Lake and can safely say it is an excellent trail, abundance of feed the entire distance and a road any fairly good pack horse could carry three hundred pounds and upwards. It is a short and easy trip to the Stickeen. Those going this trail could outfit at Ashcroft, Clinton, 150 Mile House, Soda Creek, Quesnelle and Hazleton at very moderate prices. I fear this is far from what you want in the way of information, however, it is reliable and may help you a little.

"Soda Creek, October 19, 1897."

From John King, Spokane, Wash.:

John King, a miner well known in Spokane, who has prospected and explored in the Black Hills, Arizona, Nevada, and was identified with the early history of the Coeur d'Alenes, spent two months this year on the headwaters of the Yukon, in the Cassiar and other districts. He was within 200 mi... of Klondike, and among other things says: "I was within 250 miles of the Klondike diggings, on Teslin Lake, which is the chief source of the Yukon river. The chances of getting to Klondike down that lake and the Hootalinqua River are most excellent. From Telegraph Creek the route is by pack train and horses across table lands, teeming with grass and well wooded and watered, to Tes-lin Lake, which is a large body of water. There are no high mountains by this route. Down Tes-lin Lake the journey of 200 miles to the Hootalinqua river is made in Indian canoes or boats built by the passengers themselves. From there the journey is made in the same canoes down the Hootalinqua River into the Yukon and thence to Klondike, a distance from the lake of 150 miles.

"There are few white men in the Cassiar diggings now, but those there heard of the Klondike excitement before I left. The abandoned placer mines in that district have fallen into the hands of Chinamen, as has been the case in other districts on this continent. I landed in the Cassiar country the 10th of May of this year, and work was then progressing on placer diggings. The season does not end there until the 1st of November. The climate is not half as bad as painted. The cold is intense in the winter, of course, but it is a dry cold and there are no winds to cut and bite. The Hudson's Bay Company turns out its cayuses all Winter, and in the Spring they are fat and strong. There is grass in plenty for the animals, which paw and root the thin covering of snow away and get at the feed. The Diamond S. company has mules and is obliged to cut hay for its animals in the Winter time. Trading posts are established along the trail from Telegraph Creek to Tes-lin Lake. The government built the trail and it is a good one you may be sure. Horses are not plentiful as a good cayuse sells for $150. This is because the two trading companies have a monopoly of the furnishing of supplies and own nearly all the animals. They are the freighters and packers for all the inhabitants. In that country there are plenty of cariboo, moose and black bear. Fish abound in myriads. In Tes-lin Lake salmon weighing as much as forty pounds are captured, and most of the mountain streams have trout in abundance. A few grouse and pheasant are occasionally shot, but the great game bird of that country is the ptarmigan of which there are countless thousands at times.

"I know of white men who have lived thirty years in that section and have grown children. It is a mistake to believe that the country is not inhabitable. The Diamond S. company has a trading post at the head of Teslin Lake. All its goods are brought over the government trail from the head of the navigation on the Stikeen. Early this Spring the company tried the experiment of sending three barges laden with freight and provisions down the lake and rivers to the Klondike post. Indians were placed in charge. The barges were safely landed at their destination and the Indians returned. When asked if the water route was safe they told the post traders that there was no more danger than on the Stikeen, and that steamers could run as well as barges.

"The man who goes to the Klondike by this route is exposed to few more hardships than in any new country. He will not be obliged to walk at all. He can go nearly every foot of the way on train, steamer, horse and small boat. Once at the head of navigation, the man with an outfit can employ Indians to do the drudgery of camp life and will be sure of safe pilots. The Indians, Taltons and Stikeens, get $2 a day and board. They do the cooking, set up the camp and perform all other duties. All the prospector or voyager is expected to do is to get off his horse, the Indians do the rest at night and in the morning.

"My property in that district consists of quartz claims. I am going back in two weeks by the route I have described. My principal place of operation will be on the Hootalinqua River. Should I decide to go to Klondike it will be an easy matter to get down the river to the Yukon. As I remarked before, the Indians say there are no dangerous rapids by this route. I believe it will be the future road to the Klondike."

ASHCROFT AND THOMPSON RIVER

From James Orr, of Cariboo.

F Cariboo and its mines much was heard in early days, but until the past three or four years but little since 1875. The mines that had produced so richly before and up to that dat. were about worked out, and the extreme cost of living with the high freight rates, the fact that it required heavy pumps to keep the shafts clear of water that it was necessary to sink in order to work to advantage in the old creek beds, and the further fact that most of the miners being of an adventurous disposition had moved on to Ominica and Cassiar caused Cariboo mines to be largely deserted. That there is yet untold millions in that section no one at all familiar with the country can doubt, and each year now adds to the promise of an old-time revival of the gold mining of from '59 to '75.

The personal experience of Mr. James Orr, one of Cariboo's old-timers, is well worth hearing. Landing at Williams Creek in 1862, when the famous creek was in its glory as a producer. Gold, gold, gold everywhere. Mr. Orr was one of the owners in the Caledonia and was bookkeeper for the company. In fifteen months they took out over half a million dollars. They took out $6,500 from five pans of gravel, the prize pan being $1,680. This was in 1863. Out of the Caledonia, which was sixty-seven feet to bedrock, the best paying dirt was about two feet on bedrock and the run was often 150 feet wide. The Never Sweat was adjoining and washed up every day from 60 to 200 ounces; Beauraguard as high as 800 ounces a day; New York from 150 to 200 ounces; Moffet's over $300,000 taken out of 100 feet square, which was the size of the Cariboo claims. The McLear claim was next, but not so rich. The Tinker with 300 feet of ground paid in dividends over $700,000. The Watty, a small claim next, paid $80,000. The Cameron claims cleaned up over $1,000,000; the Rabby $900,000; Dead Broke $70,000. Below were some short, but rich claims. Prince of Wales paid 8 interests half a million. Above the Caledonia, the Lillooet and Cariboo were very rich. The Aurora, with its 14 interests, paid in dividends, after all expenses were paid, about $39,000 per interest. On the Diller, two men working on the windlass and two underground took out in ten hours 102 pounds of gold. In all over $300,000 was paid in dividends to the three interests in this claim. Above the Black Jack, which was rich, the Windup was a rich fraction. From Canyon to Prince of Wales, on up to the sawmill, the Ericson, Nigger and others paid from $25,000 to $50,000 to the interest. Dozens of other claims along old Williams Creek paid enormously and the creek never received, says Mr. Orr, credit for nearly all of its enormous output, it being generally said that the sum of $25,000,000 was taken out of 1½ miles. Mr. Orr says it was twice that amount. In any case it was such a creek as was never before struck, and so far the Klondike is not in the race for record output. Other creeks in the neighborhood, Mr. Orr says, will yet prove as rich perhaps as Williams Creek was. Lightning Creek, Swift River, Slough Creek, Willow River and dozens of other creeks which have never been bottomed, will yet give up their hoard of gold. Of Omenica, Mr. Orr, who spent two years there, says it was barely scratched, and the whole of the Cassiar country is yet comparatively virgin ground. The enormous cost of provisions, difficulty of access and cost of labor all combined to make the gold hunters drop any work that would not quickly and enormously repay. To day there is no better gold country to prospect than from Cariboo through to Klondide. From Ashcroft through it is only a little over 1,200 miles, of which the first 220 miles is by a first-class wagon road, the next 560 by trail, and the balance by a splendid water course down Tes-lin Lake and the Hootalinqua River. But within one year the excitement will very likely be centered in the Cassiar range of mountains, from which water sheds the sources of the Yukon largely spring. For prospectors who wish to go in cheap we say, start from Ashcroft in April, leave Quesnelle in early May and you can spend the season most profitably in prospecting through to Telegraph Creek. If you should wish you can then sell your pack animals, for which there is always a demand at that point, and build a boat, and in a week from the time you leave Lake Tes-lin you can be at that now most talked-of spot on earth, Klondike.

THE STICKEEN ROUTE.

Captain of the Alaskan Comes Down on the City of Seattle.

CAPTAIN J. D. TACKABERY, master of the steamer Alaskan, the only steamer on the Stickeen River, speaks from experience, having navigated the river for years. In his opinion, the Stickeen-Teslin Lake route is the one route to the Yukon, and his opinion is being borne out by the fact that hundreds of men are flocking to Wrangel from Skagway and Dyea, to await the opening of the river in the spring. Some years the river is open by the latter part of April, or between the first and sixteenth of May. He has never seen it later than the latter date. It remains navigable until October, when the ice commences to come down. On the last trip of the Alaskan some ice was encountered, but since then the weather has been warmer, which might again clear the river. The Alaskan is a rather deep draught boat for river traffic, so she cannot run as long as could lighter draught steamers.

Captain Tackabery advises men not to attempt to go up the river on the ice. It is, he says, a very hard and hazardous trip, and there is not much to be gained by it. Men are still at work on the trail from Telegraph Creek to Teslin Lake. There are 300 men at Telegraph Creek waiting for the snow to fall so that they can get their goods over on sleds. Frank Yorke is taking his goods to the top of the knoll, four miles from Telegraph Creek, so that when the snow falls he will have a down grade run to the lake. There will be considerable traffic over the trail this winter, so that the snow road should be a good one.

Before leaving Telegraph Creek, Captain Tackaberry had a conversation with Mr. St. Cyr, the government engineer. Mr. St. Cyr says the route is a good one for either a wagon road or a railway. There is a very slight grade from Telegraph Creek to what is known as the top of the hill, a distance of four miles. From there to the lake is four miles.

There are a number of men coming up the river in small boats, but they, Captain Tackabery says, will never get through to Telegraph Creek, unless the ice is very late in forming. They will have to camp along the river.

CLIMATIC CONDITION.

The following report on the climatic conditions of a portion of the country through which the old telegraph trail passes and its possibilities as an agricultural country is of interest. It is taken from the report on agriculture issued by the government of British Columbia in 1896. Of the country from Ashcroft to Quesnelle it is sufficient to say that no finer farms or, as they are called, ranches, can be found in the world than the Williams Lake Ranch, the Onward Ranch, the Vieth and the Borlund's Ranch, Dunleavy's, the Australian's, Bohanon's, W. A. Johnson's, the Adams and Morrison, and scores of others found along the Cariboo road or on the Fraser and Thompson rivers. Along the lake stream luscious fruits, splendid vegetables and anything grown in almost any country, and the dry air of the Thompson valley, health-giving and pure, the mild winter with rarely any snow all goes to make this section a most desirable one for a home:

PACK TRAIN LEAVING 150 MILE HOUSE FOR SKENK RIVER

SODA CREEK AND ALEXANDRIA.

Soda Creek and Alexandria lie along the Fraser river and the Cariboo wagon road. The valley of the Fraser, above Soda Creek, widens out considerably so that the ranches are much nearer the level of the river than they are lower down; most of the ranches are on the eastern side of the river, on the Cariboo road, some of them very fine ones, notably the Australian and Bohanon's, beyond Alexandria, where extensive and profitable operations are carried on. On the western side above Alexandria are also some large fertile farms, including that of Mr. Adams, M. P. P., upon which very heavy crops of cereals are grown.

P. C. Dunlevy, Soda Creek, reports: All roots and vegetables grown; potatoes yield about 300 bushels per acre; frost injures crops in higher lands in July; droughts very often interfere with crops; irrigation being required to successfully grow heavy crops; timothy and clover are the only grasses grown for fodder, which, if mixed, are the best for cattle; alfalfa has proved successful where tried; hops grow well, but there is no consumption; cattle are kept exclusively for beef; no dairying; horses are only profitably raised in a small way, many already in the business, as a rule, only undesirable animals are raised; the ranges are abundant, and there is excellent feed from the 1st of May until the middle of November, after which ordinary cattle must be fed; sheep raising is not carried on to any extent, but the country is well adapted for the business; most farmers raise a few pigs; there is money to be made in the industry; does not pay to raise much poultry; bees have never been tried, think the summer season is too short; only small groups of good timber are to be found, as a rule there is little more than is required for general purposes; improved farms, including agricultural implements, bring from $10 to $15 per acre.

QUESNELLE.

Quesnelle is situated at the confluence of the stream of that name with the Fraser, and at the point where the Cariboo wagon road leaves the Fraser and goes in an Easterly direction to Barkerville. Barkerville is purely a mining town and the principal centre of the Cariboo mining district, one of the largest and most important in the Province. There are public schools situated both at Barkerville and Quesnelle.

Mr. R. Parkinson reports:—Wheat is grown to a limited extent; spring varieties succeed best; barley only grown for home consumption, but does well; oats are the staple crop, and demand exceeds the supply; rye is grown with success both for grain and hay; peas grow well; corn is grown only for table use, the season being too short to ripen the grain; light crops on account of the unusual season; all roots and vegetables do well; potatoes are the staple crop, they were slightly damaged by frost at the end of August; timothy is the only kind of grass grown here, price $50 per ton; crab apples and most small fruits do well.

Dairying is not carried on to any extent, no one keeps more than one cow at a time for that purpose; the price of fodder in the winter prevents farmers from keeping milch cows or making butter except in summer; there are very few sheep in the district; there are very few swine or poultry on account of the price of feed; irrigation is very necessary.

There is any amount of Government land open for pre-emption, but there is little of it of much use without irrigation, and generally the altitude is too great to allow of successful farming; it is only near the river that land is being worked at present. I know of no farms for sale here.

NECHACO.

Many inquiries have been made about the Nechaco Districts, and consequently all the information possible has been obtained from all sources. The information is somewhat contradictory, and without personal and definite knowledge of the conditions which exist there, it is impossible to give advice as to its desirability as a place for settlement. That it is a good summer stock range is unquestionable, and from all accounts there seems to be every reason to believe that a sufficiency of fodder can be produced from the natural meadows to winter stock. Its northerly position (about 54.10 N. and 124.10 W.) and its altitude, probably between 2,000 and 3,000 feet above the sea level, would naturally render it somewhat uncertain for the growing of grain crops. Still, with cultivation and drainage, it may be susceptible to great improvement in the matter of summer frosts, which has been the experience in other places with similar characteristics. In any case, situated as it is, it is evidently not a country suitable for a man with a family and small means, and unless a settler is willing to live in an isolated condition, without any immediate prospects of roads, bridges, schools, postal facilities and other adjuncts of ordinary living, he is not advised to attempt it at present. If a colony of fifty or more were to settle there, it would be somewhat different, as conditions would be altered and the lack of facilities referred to would naturally soon be obviated. The present isolated condition is undoubtedly the reason that so few settlers have thus far taken up lands there. With railway communication, however, and access to the mines of Cariboo, many of the real or alleged difficulties in existence there would no doubt soon disappear, and a very large area of pastoral and agricultural lands would be added to the wealth-producing power of the Province.

In answer to inquiries, the following letter was received from Mr. H. S. St. Laurent, Mouth of the Quesnelle:

Mr. Bowron has requested me to give you a description of the Nechaco country with reference to its capabilities for agriculture. I am not competent to give the required information. I have asked Mr. Williams, who has a ranche in the valley, and who planted some grain and vegetables this spring, and he has been good enough to give me the inclosed information. He mentioned L. A. Poudrier, D. L. S., who surveyed that valley, and he thinks that he made a correct report to the government. (See the maps and report of 1891.)

The best route to reach Nechaco is by way of Quesnelle. It is only 110 miles from here and on a good trail. The trail could be made a sleigh road at very little expense. The Black Water River and Mud River would require to be bridged. The drawback to that country is that there is no market for produce. The Indians at Stoney Creek are raising as good vegetables as we do at Quesnelle. I was told that at Fraser Lake the H. B. Co. are raising oats and vegetables as good as in any part of British Columbia.

The following is Mr. J. F. Williams' report:—A report on the Nechaco country, a general description of the country, such as the soil, water, timber, capabilities for agriculture and pastoral purposes, altitude, climate, summer frost, the possibility of grain-raising and vegetables, any swamps to make hay, the time the spring opens. In regard to the above questions, I will answer as far as I know. Spring begins about the latter part of March and the first of April. The soil is very rich and productive.

All root vegetables grow in abundance; berry fruits grow immense. I have never seen a better oat and barley crop grow than I had on nine acres last year (1895). I am told there had been good wheat raised by the H. B. Co. some years ago. It is subject to summer frost, more or less, but no more than other localities in British Columbia where they raise good grain. Good water is plentiful over all the country. Heavy timber is not so plenty, only in the foothills.

Small timber grows over all the country, cottonwood, birch and black willow; the feed and grass is growing over the whole country, but it could not be called a first-class stock country, though there are plenty of large swamps that make fine hay meadows.

There could be a first-class wagon road made with little expense from Quesnelle to Nechaco, that would be about 110 miles; a good trail and right of way is already made from this point to Nechaco, and the winters are not severe on stock, as they winter through without hay most winters. I am able to say, moreover, that I am going back this spring to seed ten acres more and break about forty acres more new land, and improve some more. Anyone to read Mr. L. A. Poudrier's report about the country will find that he describes it very truthfully. There is as fine water power of a good many thousand inches as a person could wish for just about the center of the country, viz., the Stoney Creek Falls, about a mile and a half from the Nechaco River. The country in the vicinity of the Falls is comparatively level, and it could easily be farmed; the soil is very rich, with a heavy growth of grass and hay.

KLONDIKE.

Of Klondike, where such a man as Wm. Ogilvie says, as he did in a report made by himself for the Canadian government in which he states that there is now practically more than $60,000,000 in sight on Bonanza and Eldorado creeks alone, with a section of country stretching from Cariboo clear through to Klondike that is not prospected. It means that hundreds of thousands will find profitable employment for fifty years to come in this vast area.

Joaquin Miller says:

"The gold is here, and let me finally repeat the room is here, but there is room for men only, men with heads and hearts, and spine and marrow, and they must come equipped. Here is room for not only thousands, but hundreds of thousands on mining grounds already discovered. I am quite responsible for this assertion, although I have heard it since from many men. Some of them thought that suffering might come of it; others, selfish in the wish to get plenty of ground and gold in their own hands before strangers can get here. I have entered into every camp here, looked into every big claim, talked to every miner. I have set down the facts as I have found them. I leave you to form your own conclusions, to decide and to do as you please."

Mr. Harry de Windt in *The Strand* of November, says:

"As to the great Klondike 'rush' next spring there is no doubt it will alter the face of the entire region, the climate notwithstanding. Railways and steamships and telegraphs will soon be established. Fortunes will be

MAP SHOWING OVERLAND ROUTE

made, and the unlucky forced to the wall. Sensational reports may be
expected daily, for the place is a real Tom Tiddler's ground, honeycombed
by rivers and creeks with sauds of gold. There is plenty of room for all
between the Klondike to the Cassiar. Let the gold-seekers take their time
and make prudent preparations. The ultimate result will doubtless be that a
little known region will be dotted with thriving cities, and the shouts of
triumph from the fortunate few will drown the dying wails of the many who
will fail."

LILLOOET.

The prominence of this section is owing to its immensely valuable quartz
mines that have within the past few months been more prominently brought
before the public than ever before. The Golden Cache mines, the Ben D.
Orr group and numerous others show great values. The entire country will,
next season, be alive with prospectors, and there is an unlimited field. To
reach Lillooet, a good wagon road from Ashcroft, distance 60 miles. There
is also a trail up the Fraser from Lytton.

LYTTON.

At the junction of the Thompson with the Fraser River, is a thriving village surrounded with good quartz ledges, and is a good field for prospectors.
It is distant from Ashcroft about 50 miles west. Kamloops being the same
distance east of Ashcroft. All places being on the Canadian Pacific Railroad.

KAMLOOPS.

Kamloops is a beautifully situated little city at the junction of the North
and East Thompson Rivers, and at the head of Kamloops Lake. There are
about 2,000 people residing there. It is a railroad divisional point and is a
growing, thriving place. Many prospectors going up the Cariboo Road to
the Northern gold fields, will buy their horses and outfits at this point.
There is a good wagon road leading from Kamloops to Cache Creek and
Ashcroft. Its merchants are a lively lot of people that keep apace of the
times. It has two newspapers, the *Sentinel* and the *Standard*, both are up
to date and are of great assistance in making the resources of the interior
and Northern British Columbia known to the world at large. Kamloops has
quartz mines of great value in its immediate neighborhood, principally gold
and copper, also coal and iron.

ASHCROFT.

On the Canadian Pacific Railroad, 203 miles East of Vancouver, and in
the valley formed by the Thompson River, a healthy pleasant village of about
400 people, good stores and good hotels. The mild and pleasant winters
make the towns of Ashcroft and Kamloops desirab'e places in which to pass
the winter, from the fact that 1,000 horses are continually freighting goods
from Ashcroft to different points along the Cariboo road and to the different
mining camps of the interior it is a lively town, and rapidly putting on
metropolitan airs. Water works, and electric lights will be put in yet this
season. Many hundreds of men will pass at least a portion of the winter at

Ashcroft gathering information about the upper country. It is now thoroughly understood that the Overland Telegraph Line will be extended from Quesnelle to Dawson City next season. This will make Ashcroft the distributing point for all Klondike news, and a telegraphic center. Of fruits and potatoes Ashcroft can beat the world, for stock the surrounding ranches can give a good account of themselves. The Western Canadian Ranching Company owns not less than 10,000 head of cattle. John Wilson, of Ashcroft, is known the Province through as the cattle king. He owns or controls several ranches and many thousand head of cattle.

British Columbia on the whole is prosperous, and good settlers, those that will make desirable citizens, are in demand, none others need apply.

THE KISGAGASH DISTRICT.

The Kisgagash district, situated on the route from Ashcroft to the Yukon, about sixty miles from Hazelton, sends out reports of recent good strikes. J. D. Devereaux, representative of the *Mining Journal*, writing from Hazelton about the Kisgagash country, says:

"I have seen ore from thirteen claims in the Kisgagash district which all look to be very highly mineralized. Some of it is known to run as high as $200 to $300 to the ton in gold alone, and, by information given me by the miners, the cream of the country is not touched yet. All the old experienced hands say that the Kisgagash country will be a better camp than the Kootenay ever can expect to be, as they have gold, silver, copper and lead, where the Kootenay is mostly silver, which is falling in value every day. Little or nothing is known about the wealth of this country by the outside world. Within the past five years I venture to say that $250,000 has been taken out of this country by individual miners, mostly Chinese."

Intending parties heading for the Klondike, and who take the overland route, would do well to prospect this part of the country. As is well known, and is verified by all who have been in the northern districts, that by going over the old telegraph trail good mineral can be found almost anywhere. The great influx of people next spring will open up these districts adjacent to Cariboo, and it is quite probable that some will strike a nice Klondike nearer home.

The following is the report of the Old Telegraph Trail from Quesnelle to Hazelton by J. D. Devereaux, Representative of the B. C. "Mining Journal." Mr. Devereaux left Quesnelle September 7th and arrived at Hazleton September 19th, making the trip in good time.

HAZLETON, B. C., September 22.

SIR: Complying with your instructions dated September 2d, I immediately made arrangements for the trip from Quesnelle to Teslin Lake via the old telegraph trail.

I hereby submit my report of the condition of the trail between Quesnelle and Hazleton, the feed thereon and the feasibility of a road being opened up to the aforesaid place.

On the 7th inst. I started and traveled on a splendid trail to the 12 Mile Camp, where feed was in abundance. Pushing on I arrived at Goose Lake (or 25 Mile Camp), where a halt was made for the day. Feed very plentiful and trail in good condition.

8th. Started early, passed 36 Mile Camp at 9:15; feed good. Arrived at Blackwater at 2:50, where camp was made for the day. The present locality cannot be improved upon for a road (with exception of the descent to the Blackwater).

9th. Traveled over a good trail for 17 miles to Mud River, feed plentiful but a dreaded camp to packers owing to the present state of crossing facilities. This may be avoided by cutting a road further west, and by bridging the Mud River canyon, which is very narrow. On the other side the trail is good with exception of a few mud holes near Lost Horse Meadows, 10 miles from Mud River. Went on to the south end of Nathelby's Lake, where good feed abounds, and camped, covering 30 miles for the day.

10th. Trail very rough for 4 miles along Nathelby's Lake, but as soon as the trail leaves the lake and strikes high ground it becomes good again to the north end of Bobtail Lake, where good feed is found. Continuing for the first two miles a few mud holes are found, but can be easily avoided. The balance of the day's travel to Tsin-Cut Lake was over a good trail with a few exceptions, where it was found very brushy. There is an abundance of feed here, principally peavine. The distance traveled for the day was 34 miles, most of the way being quite suitable for a road bed.

11th. Traveled all day over a very good trail (patches of prairie land intervening every three or four miles) to the crossing of the Nechaco, 37 miles from Tsin-Cut Lake, where swimming must be resorted to in order to cross. This can easily be avoided by bridging the canyon 1½ miles below. The canyon is narrow, and further, has an island in the center very suitable for a road.

13th. Traveled through partly open country until 2 o'clock, then through 4 miles heavy timber to prairie again. Camped on the south end of Burn's Lake or the head of the Endako River. Covered 28 miles.

14th. Traveled through comparatively open country all day. Feed very plentiful; camped on the extreme head of the Fraser River water shed. Covered 20 miles.

15th. One mile's travel brought me to the divide, where feed begins to get scarce, but plentiful enough for grazing purposes until I reached Elwyn Lake, where I made camp for the day, having covered 22 miles.

I would advise that a new road be cut on the north side of the divide. By doing so more feed can be taken in, and also avoid the two crossings of the Buckley River, which are very troublesome in the spring.

16th. Made a late start, traveled all day through partly open country, camped on a large prairie at night. Traveled 18 miles.

17th. Traveled along side hill until 10:20; open country with good feed. A gradual descent for two miles into level country where a better place for a road cannot be found. Camped on a small prairie with peavine and blue joint growing as high as the horses. Covered 28 miles.

18th. Traveled all day through level country and splendid feed; crossed the Mauricetown at 12:15. Camped at night on what the Mauricetown Indians call the Halfway prairie. Traveled 23 miles.

SCENES AT QUESNELL, B.C.

19th. Made an early start and arrived at Hazleton at 10:30, after traveling 12 miles over a good trail. Here we once more find a Hudson's Bay
Company's store, where the greatest kindness is shown to travelers by the
genial manager, R. S. Sargent.

The approximate distance between Hazleton and Quesnelle is 227 miles.

TELEGRAPH LINE TO DAWSON.

Among the guests at the Palace Hotel is C. R. Hosmer, general manager
of the Canadian Pacific Telegraph Company, with headquarters at Montreal,
and who also holds the position of general manager of the Pacific Postal
Telegraph Company, and vice-president of the Commercial Cable Company,
says the San Francisco *Chronicle*. He has been in the Northwest for some
days past, looking into the proposition now contemplated by the Dominion
government of building a telegraph line to the Klondike, and he brings the
information that the line will be built and in operation early in the coming
year. From Victoria, Mr. Hosmer came from San Francisco to see John W.
Mackay, and he spent most of the day yesterday in Mr. Mackay's company.
He expects to remain here until the end of the week, when he will leave for
Montreal by way of the Canadian Pacific.

"There is no doubt," he said last evening, "but that the proposed line
to Dawson will be built during the coming spring. And what is most interesting to contemplate is the fact that the line will be stretched over the same
country that was traversed with a telegraph line thirty years ago. It has
been determined by recent surveys that the only practicable route for the
new line is over the same route that was surveyed and partly wired in 1866
and 1867, in the attempt to secure telegraphic communication with the continent on the other side of the water.

"As everyone doubtless knows, for this is a matter of history — a telegraph line was built some distance north on this side of the continent at that
time, while another force was engaged in building a line on the Siberian
coast. The two lines were to be connected with a cable forty miles long
through Behring Sea, and the work was progressing favorably, when the
successful laying of the first Atlantic cable caused the entire project to be
abandoned. Now, after a lapse of thirty years, the project, or part of it at
least, is to be revived, and I would not be surprised to see the line extended
in the not far distant future from Dawson City to the Alaskan coast at some
point about St. Michaels, and a connecting cable laid under the waters of
Behring Sea. If this were done only 150 miles of connecting line would
have to be built to connect with the telegraph line of the Trans Siberian
Railway.

"While in Vancouver I met Clifford Sifton, the Canadian minister of the
interior, who had just returned from a trip over the Chilkoot and White
passes, whereat he went to take a look at the country through which the
telegraph line will be built. I believe this line will be built in the very near
future, and our company will operate it. The expenditure will probably not
exceed $300,000 or $400,000. The line will run from Ashcroft, on the line of
the Canadian Pacific, in a northerly direction through Quesnelle to Dawson,
a distance of 1,400 miles. For the greater part of the distance the line will

traverse a timbered country, which will greatly expedite the work of construction and reduce the cost to a minimum. When it is completed there is every probability that connecting lines will be built to Juneau and other points of importance in Alaska and the Northwest Territory, and there is every indication that such lines, with the big volume of the traffic that will start northward in the spring, would be paying investments from the start."

MINING LICENSES.

The attention of all intending to go to the Northern gold fields is called to the fact that a duty of 30 per cent. is collected on all goods brought into Canada, or any part of it, that the gold fields are principally in Canada, and that goods can be bought as cheaply and of as good grade at Ashcroft, Kamloops or Vancouver as at any place in the States or in British Columbia. There are liberal laws for miners. All nationalities stand alike. There are no large royalties to pay, and no reservation of alternate claims. The mining regulations are not published in this volume for the Northwest territory, for the reason that new regulations will be promulgated early in the winter, they will be liberal and specific. Prospectors will be able to obtain a license for prospecting in both British Columbia and the Northwest Territories at Ashcroft. The former costs $5 and the latter $15 for one year. Direct railroad connection is made with Ashcroft by way of the Chicago, Milwaukee and St. Paul, the Soo Line, and the Canadian Pacific. Through rates are made, and through tickets sold at the offices of any of the above named roads. For any further information write to the advertisers whose notices are found in this volume.

By subscribing for the B. C. Mining Journal, published every Saturday at Ashcroft, B. C., those desiring further information of the Ashcroft route, who travels it, etc., can obtain reliable information.

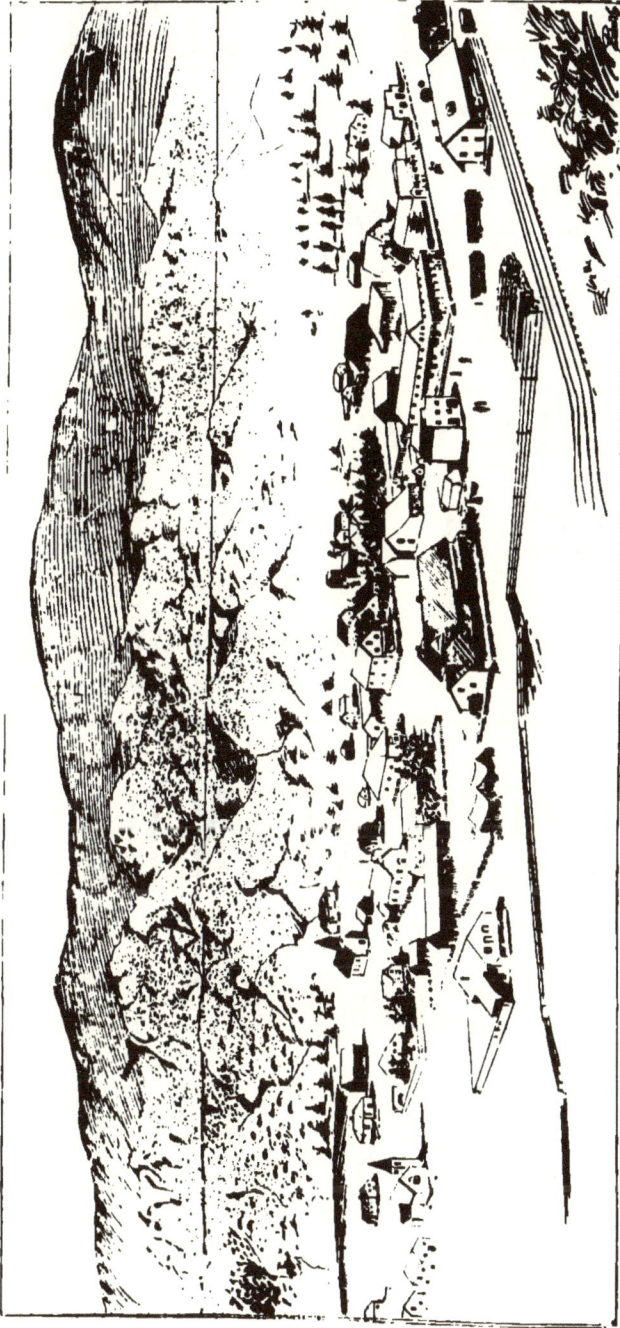

ASHCROFT, B. C.

83 MILE HOUSE

Stages Each Way Stop Over Night

First-Class Accommodation for Guests. Good Bar in Connection. Good Stabling and Feed for Horses

❊ ❊

CARIBOO ROAD, B. C.

McTAVISH & CO., Proprietors

COSMOPOLITAN HOTEL

Kamloops, B. C.

Good Stabling in Connection

J. H. RUSSELL & H. HEROD, Props.

150 Mile House

The distributing point for all the
Hydraulic Mines at
Horse Fly, North and South Forks and
main Quesnelle River, also the
Stock Ranges of
Chilcoten and Beaver Lake Valley.
At this point will be found a
good assortment of

General

Merchandise and

Miners' Supplies

Also one of the best hotels
on the route.
Information cheerfully given.

Vehit & Borland

Proprietors
and Stock Raisers

Pither & Leiser

I. LEHMAN

Hudson's Bay Co.

**Quesnelle Mouth,
Cariboo,
B. C.**

Direct Importers and
Dealers in

Wines, Liquors and Cigars

Dry Goods & Groceries
HARDWARE & & &
BOOTS and SHOES

Miners' Supplies

Bed Rock
Prices
Goods Guaranteed
Quality
Guaranteed

Quesnelle
Cariboo
Yukon

**Recognizing
Quesnelle
to be
the Center
of the
Great Mining
Belt
of British
Columbia
and the Yukon in the Northwest Territory**

The undersigned has always on hand a superior stock of Groceries, Dry Goods, Boots and Shoes, Hardware. Miners' Supplies of all kinds. Flour, Beans and Bacon of the best. Lumber, rough and dressed. Saw Mill to cut lumber to sizes required. Shingles, pine and cedar. ❧ ❧

**Special attention given to outfit=
ting parties enroute for
Ominica, Peace River and the Yukon**

Prices Right❧

JAMES REID.

F. W. FOSTER

General Merchant

Ashcroft Station and Clinton, B. C.

Keeps Constantly on Hand

Full Outfits

for Miners and

Prospectors

Prices Right

Enquiries by Mail Concerning ..... Klondike and other Gold Mining Camps promptly answered

F. W. FOSTER...Ashcroft, B.C.

Cariboo and Lillooet

Stage Travel

British Columbia Express Co.
Ltd.

STUDEBAKER

WAGONS

McCormick's Binders and Mowers, McClary's Famous Stoves, Farming Tools and General Hardware

James Vair, Kamloops, B.C.

B. C. Cattle Co.
Ranches CHILCOTEN, B. C.

Large bands of Cayuses for sale
broke to saddle or for packing.
Fat cattle for the northern markets for sale.

For particulars, prices, etc., address as above............

---

20 Mile House ❧

JACOB MUNDORF, Propr.

This popular house is ready at all times
to accommodate the traveling public.

20 miles from Ashcroft on Cariboo road.

Chas. Pennie-Stockman
Pennieston--B. C.

Fat Cattle for

the Overland

Drive Furnished

at Fair Prices

Philip Parkes

Bonaparte, B. C.

CATTLE for the overland drive, good stock and in good condition.

Thos. McEwen...

STOCK
RAISER

Fat Cattle for the Overland Drive   **Animals for Packing**

P. O. ADDRESS, **Dog Creek, B. C.**

Eagle & Paxton

General Merchants

Dealers in Groceries, Hardware, Dry Goods, Boots and Shoes, Crockery, Drugs, and Farm Produce

**THE CHEAPEST
CASH STORE
IN THE CARIBOO DISTRICT**

ONWARD RANCH
CARIBOO,
B. C.

The Cariboo Exchange

THIS well-known house
has been recently fitted
up by its owner,
Mr. A. H. Walters.
It is now with its
Annexes a convenient
and pleasant place to stay.
Mrs. Walters
who has charge of the
Dining Rooms
serves meals of the best
to be procured in
the country.
Rates very moderate.

A. H. Walters
Proprietor

The Ashcroft Hotel

THIS favorite and conveniently located House has been added to so that accommodations are provided for a large number of guests. Two large and commodious Annexes in connection with the House ✶✶✶✶✶✶✶

Directly opposite the C. P. R. Depot and Open Day and Night

Wm. Lyne
Proprietor

McGILIVRAY BROS.

Hotel and Feed Stables

The 59 Mile House.

CARIBOO ROAD, B. C.

Colonial Hotel and General Store

R. McLEESE, Proprietor

A full assortment of
Dry Goods,
Boots and Shoes,
Liquors, Cigars, Hardware,
Hay, Grain and
Miners' Supplies, at
Reasonable rates.

WHOLESALE AND RETAIL

SODA CREEK, B. C.

Via ❧ Steamer

Quesnelle

to Yukon "Charlotte"

❧❧❧❧❧❧

Leaves Soda Creek on arrival of mails
and express from Ashcroft for all points
to Quesnelle, connecting with boats
going to Fort George, Fort St. James on
Stuart Lake, North Tatlah Lake, the
Buckley House, Fort Conally on Bear
Lake, thence by rivers and trails to the
head waters of the Yukon; all in Canadian territory and in the gold belt all
the way from Cariboo to Klondike.

❧❧❧❧❧❧

For freight and passage apply to the purser on
board.

JAS. REID, Manager

P. C. DUNLEVY

Hotel Keeper
and
General Merchant

A GOOD stock of GOODS constantly on hand

SODA CREEK, B. C.

QUESNELLE, B. C.

The Occidental Hotel

Is the Leading Hotel
of North Cariboo.....
On your way over-
land call and see us.

JOHNSON & HOFFERCAMP
PROPRIETORS

The Cargile House

This well known house has been enlarged and refitted, and is prepared to accommodate a large number of guests

G. B. Johnson

Proprietor

Good service and good fare. Terms by the day, week or month, very moderate.

The Ashcroft, Lake Teslin and Yukon Transportation, Trading and Mining Co.

Will transport those wishing to visit the northern gold fields and will furnish them with supplies delivered at the mines, at reasonable terms.

Full details will be published soon.

For particulars, address The SECRETARY, at
Ashcroft, B. C.

FOR THE NORTHERN GOLD FIELDS

FIRST~CLASS

GOODS AT RIGHT PRICES

C. A. SEMLIN

Cache Creek

Cattle and Horses
for the
Overland
trade for
Sale

P. O
Address
Cache
Creek
B.C.

J. G. BARNES

Will Furnish Cattle
by Contract for the
Overland Trail

....The
same to be in Good Condition about May 1st

ASHCROFT, B. C.

Canadian Pacific Railway

Soo Pacific Line

To Klondike Gold Fields

IF you are going to the Klondike gold fields call on or write any agent of the Canadian Pacific Railway or Soo Pacific Line. This is our best route. There are no customs difficulties; close and direct connection made with all steamers sailing from Vancouver, Victoria, or Seattle. Rates lower than by any other line.

List of steamers sailing furnished on application, and berths on any particular steamer reserved on application.

W. R. CALLAWAY Gen. Pass. Agt., Soo Line Minneapolis, Minn.	**E. J. COYLE** Dist. Pass. Agent, Vancouver, B. C.
ROBT. KERR Traffic Mgr., Winnipeg	**D. McNICOLL** Pass. Traffic Mgr., Montreal

The Chicago, Milwaukee & St. Paul Ry.

Is the best line to and from Chicago, Milwaukee and all points East. With its 6,155 miles of thoroughly equipped road it reaches all principal centers in Northern Illinois, Wisconsin, Iowa, Minnesota, South Dakota, North Dakoka, and Northern Michigan

THE ONLY LINE

Running Electric Lighted and Steam Heated Vestibule Trains. Time tables, maps and information regarding routes, rates, and other details relating to the road will be furnished on application to any coupon ticket agent, or by addressing GEO. H. HEAFFORD, General Passenger and Ticket Agent. Chicago, Ill., or C. J. EDDY, General Agent, Portland, Oregon

www.ingramcontent.com/pod-product-compliance
Lightning Source LLC
Chambersburg PA
CBHW022152090426
42742CB00010B/1483